A Cloud of Witnesses

From Saints to Suffragettes Around Stirling

Edited by Thomas A. Christie
and Margaret L. Lovett

With Illustrations by
Catriona M. MacKenzie

ROBERT GREENE PUBLISHING
ON BEHALF OF
STIRLING CHRISTIANS TOGETHER

A Cloud of Witnesses
From Saints to Suffragettes Around Stirling

Second Edition, 2011.

ISBN-10: 0-9510602-8-7
ISBN-13: 978-0-9510602-8-5

Robert Greene Publishing
on behalf of Stirling Christians Together
Stirling
Scotland
FK9 5NR

This book is available for purchase from the following organisations:
The Stirling Smith Art Gallery and Museum, Dumbarton Road, Stirling.
The Faith Mission Bookshop, Barnton Street, Stirling.
Participating churches in the Stirling and District Area.
Selected other retail outlets.

The Ancient Seal of Stirling

"Here stand the Scots saved by the Cross"

A Cloud of Witnesses
From Saints to Suffragettes Around Stirling

Second Edition, 2011.

Printed and bound in Great Britain.
Set in Times New Roman on 10-16pt. and Raleigh SF on 36pt.

Table of Contents

Map of the City of Stirling

Stirling Castle

Barn Road

Upper Bridge Street

Queen Street

Cowane Street

Viewfield Place

Irvine Place

Argyll's Lodging

Castle Wynd

St Mary's Wynd

Princes Street

Barnton Street

Goosecroft Road

Mar's Wark

Broad Street

Tolbooth

Bow Street

Friars Street

Baker Street

Murray Place

St John Street

Old Town Jail

Spittal Street

The Back Walk

King Street

The Stirling Smith Art Gallery & Museum

The Albert Hall

Corn Exchange Road

Port Street

Albert Place

Dumbarton Road

Map of Stirling and its Surrounding Area

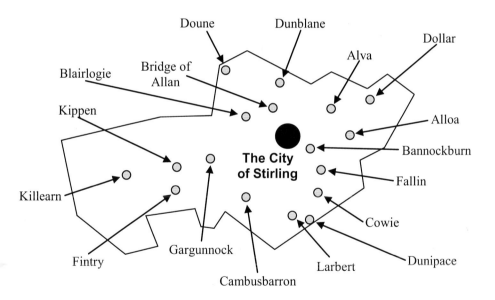

We dedicate this book to the younger generation.

'Wherefore seeing we also are compassed about with so great a cloud of witnesses, let us lay aside every weight, and the sin which doth so easily beset us, and let us run with patience the race that is set before us, looking unto Jesus the author and finisher of our faith; who for the joy that was set before him endured the cross, despising the shame, and is set down at the right hand of the throne of God.'

Hebrews 12:1-2
(The King James Bible)

Introduction

Stirling has a rich Christian Heritage: men and women, some ordinary, others extraordinary, who, by their dedication to a cause, changed the society around them.

They, like us, walked those same cobbled streets up to the ancient castle fortress and watched the sun set behind the Perthshire hills; they too followed the river, meandering dreamily past the edge of the Carse and out along the Hillfoots in the shadow of the Ochils to the busy estuary waterways of the Firth of Forth.

Recently *Stirling Christians Together* presented a dramatised version of the lives of some of our predecessors at a Pentecost Celebration in the Albert Hall. A very positive response encouraged us to produce this book.

We hope the stories will be both interesting and challenging.

* * *

With thanks to:

The Drummond Trust, 3 Pitt Terrace, Stirling for grant assistance.
Dr Ken MacKay for practical suggestions and encouragement.
Dr Elspeth King for an inspiring tour of The Valley Cemetery, and for her information and support.
Stirling Council Libraries.
All the contributors who gave freely of their time and expertise.

Margaret L. Lovett and Thomas A. Christie
Editors
Stirling, September 2011

Saint Ninian

(Fifth Century AD)

The large and historic Parish of St Ninians in Stirling takes its name from the 5th century Saint who is closely associated with Whithorn and Galloway.

The early story of St Ninians is hid in the mists of antiquity. Perhaps St Ninian in his travels north from Candida Casa in Whithorn spent some time in this territory south of the Forth. His name is certainly associated with St Ninians Well, beside the Wellgreen, and it is known that he, or his associates, sought to evangelise Scotland.

Little is actually known about Ninian himself, but it is thought that his monasticism was inspired by that of St Martin. A book in the 12th century speaks of the life, good works and kindness of the Saint, with many Churches across Scotland and beyond being dedicated to Ninian.

Historically, we do know that from the 7th century people made a pilgrimage to visit the shrine of St Ninian in Whithorn, believing in his power to cure illness and perform miracles. The town became a revered place and over

ST NINIANS WELL

many centuries both kings and commoners made the journey. As a result, the fame of Ninian and Whithorn spread. Pilgrims still visit Whithorn in order to discover the history of the town and its role in shaping the history of Scotland.

Rev. Gary McIntyre

Saint Blane

(? - 590)

St Blane, or Bláán from the old Irish, is a bit of a mystery figure; all we can do is work back from what we know to seek to establish his origins. Places that bear his name are Dunblane, Strathblane, Blanefield and St Blanes Church on the Isle of Bute. Like most of the ancient saints it is unlikely that they actually visited all or any of the places associated with their names. Most likely later followers carried the name and work of St Blane to all but the Isle of Bute.

The Aberdeen Breviary, containing a list of Celtic saints, states that Blane was educated in Ireland and came to Scotland to work amongst the Picts. This account has been challenged by later historians who suggest that he was most likely born on the Isle of Bute where he became a monk.

Celtic monks lived very disciplined lives and could choose between three different forms of martyrdom. The first level was green which meant that they chose to live a life of isolation. The second was white in which they travelled far from their home country to do mission work. The third was red in which they sought out contact with and lived among hostile heathens.

The south western end of the Isle of Bute would have been an ideal place for a Dysart, a Celtic place of isolation and meditation. They used caves or small beehive shaped stone cells for prayer and meditation. This life of isolation, rather than keeping people away, became a fascination to locals.

It is perhaps hard for us today to understand the kind of esteem and influence that such a way of life brought to someone like St Blane. Many would have been inspired and influenced by his devotion. This influence would last long after his death, and his followers would have sought to keep his memory alive by their own devotion and influence. Tradition says that St Blane died in AD 590 and was buried in Kingarth on the Isle of Bute, where a church dedicated to him now stands.

It could well have been the case that in later years, as increasing threats came from the seas around Bute in the form of a variety of marauding bands of warriors, St Blane's successors firstly moved away from the island and then from the western coast steadily moving inland to the north and east.

What is certain is that St Blane was worthy of being remembered, that he touched the lives of those who kept his name alive and sought to follow in his footsteps. His faith and devotion were the marks of his life and the inspiration to those who established religious communities and built churches. Although we know little about him, in the communities bearing his name we get an intriguing glimpse of this Celtic Saint.

Rev. Alex B. Mitchell

Saint Margaret

(1045 - 93)

Margaret, a princess of royal blood, had to flee from the English court as the Norman invasion advanced. She hurriedly set sail with her attendants, but as soon as they left the shelter of the harbour a violent storm caught the small boat driving it northwards towards Scotland.

Was Margaret's original plan to sail towards Europe and to enter a convent in her native Hungary? The fierce weather robbed her of choice. Her boat was wrecked on the coast of Fife. Weak, hungry and exhausted, clutching her most precious possessions - a Book of Gospels and a gold casket engraved with a cross - Margaret struggled ashore. She had to seek asylum in Scotland.

Malcolm III (known as Malcolm Canmore: in Gaelic, 'Big Head'), Scotland's 'warrior king', gave Margaret and her attendants a very warm welcome. She was offered a home at his royal court near Dunfermline. Malcolm, whose father King Duncan had been murdered by Macbeth, was a widower with three sons. He spent most of his time travelling around Scotland with his band of soldiers, uniting his kingdom and defending his boundaries. Malcolm's royal court was rough and ready, like rowdy barracks, compared with the sophisticated palaces of Hungary and England.

Margaret intrigued him. He had met her at the English Court when she was eleven years old. Now he saw and admired a dignified, well-educated, if somewhat serious, lady who was a devout Christian. Every night she would slip out of the castle alone. Curious, he followed her and

ROYAL WEDDING, 1070 AD

found her in a small cave nearby, praying. He had the cave made into a beautiful chapel for her.

Margaret must have suffered culture shock at her change of circumstances. As senior lady at court she quietly began to change things. New furniture and wall hangings from abroad were ordered for the rooms, and individual eating and drinking implements replaced common platters and cups.

Gradually the manners and the whole atmosphere at court began to improve. Malcolm gave his full support to all her ideas. Within a year of her arrival he had fallen in love with her, and their marriage took place amidst great national celebrations.

As Queen, Margaret's influence grew. She attempted to unite the Celtic Church and the Church of Rome. In these discussions Malcolm, believing that church unity would strengthen his kingdom, acted as Gaelic interpreter. He was well aware that not everyone approved of her changes.

Queen Margaret established Sunday as a holy day, instead of a day for revelry and trading at market. She founded a monastery at Dunfermline, purchasing from abroad beautiful church furnishings and vestments as an aid to worship. She was a patron of both the Céli De (a celtic religious order) and of the Benedictine monks she introduced from Europe. She encouraged them all in their meticulous copying of Scriptures and exquisite illustrations - so essential for the communication of the Gospel before the days of printing. Queen Margaret understood that pilgrimages could deepen spiritual life. She made the journey easier for the weary traveller by establishing free hostels and free ferry crossings for pilgrims en route to Dunfermline and St Andrews. Queensferry is named after her.

Realising the importance of education, Queen Margaret invited tutors from England to teach her seven sons, and she urged the nobles who attended court to have their sons educated also. She sent her two daughters to a convent school in England. All these links with other countries increased trade and dialogue with Europe and raised Scotland's profile abroad.

However, it is for her godly character and her kindness to the poor that Queen Margaret is remembered today. She rose early to pray and meditate, her favourite reading being the Book of Gospels. Following the Christian Service for the court, she would personally attend to the washing and feeding of the orphans and beggars who were brought to her daily. Only then would she sit down to eat. She and King Malcolm would give banquets in the main hall for groups of the poor, with the chaplain in attendance.

Archbishop Turgot of St Andrews, Margaret's priest and biographer, reckoned that Malcolm supported his wife in all her endeavours because 'he could not help seeing from her conduct that Christ dwelt within her'. Although he could neither read nor write, Malcolm revered the Scriptures and would kiss the Book of Gospels.

King Malcolm had a great castle built in Edinburgh for his Queen and growing family. From time to time, despite his wife's misgivings, he would engage in battle in defence of his border territories. Queen Margaret had become ill and was lying in bed in Edinburgh Castle when news was brought to her that her husband and eldest son had been killed in action. Heartbroken, she died soon afterwards, aged forty-six years.

In recognition of her godly life, Margaret was declared a saint in 1246. She is commemorated in St Margaret's Chapel at Edinburgh Castle.

In Stirling, Queen Margaret gifted land near the Castle for educational use. The old Stirling High School, which was built on the site, had St Margaret on the school badge. The school building is now the Highland Hotel. On November 10th every year, St Margaret's Catholic Church in Stirling has a celebration to mark her life and influence.

Margaret L. Lovett

Saint David

(1083 - 1153)

As ninth son of King Malcolm III, David I was low in the line of succession to the throne, but by 1124 he was crowned King of Scotland.

Although he had no expectation of being king, David was not unprepared. From frequent visits to his extensive estates in England he had developed a growing interest in Norman government and architecture. His father had taught him the skills of a warrior, and his mother, Queen Margaret, had ensured that he received a good education and that he was well versed in the Christian religion.

There is a story told that, while out hunting near Arthur's Seat in Edinburgh, King David was thrown from his horse and a huge stag wheeled round to gore him. As he held out his arm to shield his face from attack, there appeared, between the stag's antlers, a vision of the Cross. The stag leapt away, and David escaped unharmed. In gratitude to God he later built a church on the site - the Church of the Holy Rude (Holy Cross). Today we can see this event commemorated in the stag's head and cross on the top of Canongate Kirk in Edinburgh's Royal Mile.

King David continued his mother's mission to expand the influence of Christianity in Scotland. He surrounded himself with advisers from the Church. With their help and assistance he established a string of monasteries throughout the land, from Kinloss in the North to Jedburgh in the South, including Cambuskenneth Abbey in Stirling. These were stone-built and of elaborate Norman architecture. During this period a seminary was built in Stirling at the Top of the Town. The old High School, now the Highland Hotel, replaced the original building.

King David I also granted Royal Burgh status to Stirling, thus enhancing the trading opportunities and the discipline in the town.

David I was the only Scottish king who was also a saint. As he had granted so much land and wealth to the Church at the expense of the Crown, King James I would later call him the 'Sair Saint for the Crown'.

Margaret L. Lovett

CAMBUSKENNETH ABBEY

Thomas Forret

(d.1538/40)

Thomas Forret was one of the dedicated pre-Reformation clergy who attempted to reach out to the spiritual and pastoral needs of his flock, but he came into conflict with the Church authorities for preaching and teaching in the English language. William Tyndale's translation had made access to the Bible possible for those who could not read Latin, but the Church was unwilling to accept the risks of personal judgement and 'error' that might result, and so the reading of Scriptures in English was prohibited in 1536.   Eventually Forret was executed for refusing to compromise his passion for spreading the Gospel in ways people could understand easily.

Forret was a well-educated canon of the Augustinian priory of Inchcolm on the Firth of Forth. Like Luther and Calvin, he was influenced by the works of St Augustine, and exclaimed, "O happy and blessed was that book by which I came to the knowledge of the truth". Forret became vicar of Dollar, and set about preaching the New Testament Epistles and Gospels to his flock in English.   Realising that they also needed instruction, he taught them the Ten Commandments, the Creed and the Lord's Prayer in English, and composed a simple catechism.   Forret is also believed to have had the original 'Vicar's Bridge' built over the River Devon a mile or so from Dollar.

In many ways, Forret was a devoted pastor, who not only studied the Bible assiduously himself (learning three chapters of Romans a day in Latin), but who also took bread and cheese to the needy and refused to demand the 'best cow and uppermost cloth' of those deceased as his due. But his very dedication brought him into disrepute, as it showed up other clergy who were less exemplary, and aroused the hostility of the friars who thought that preaching was their special gift.

George Crichton, the Bishop of Dunkeld, tackled Forret about all this, and suggested he preach only on 'one good Epistle or one good Gospel'.

CASTLE CAMPBELL, DOLLAR

Forret replied that he had never found any evil epistle or gospel in the New or Old Testament. The Bishop said he himself knew nothing about the Old and New Testaments and just kept to his service books. He admonished Forret, "Leave those fancies, or else you may repent of them when it is too late".

Eventually, the authorities ran out of patience with Forret, and Cardinal David Beaton, Bishop of Glasgow, and Bishop Crichton summoned him to answer charges of heresy along with two friars, a priest called Duncan Sympson from Stirling, and several others including Robert Foster, a 'gentleman', also from Stirling. At his trial, Forret used 1 Corinthians 14:19 to justify using an English Bible: "I would rather speak five words that make sense in order to instruct others also, than ten thousand in a language that others do not know". Asked to prove that this was in the Bible, he took out a New Testament in English from his coat, and this was enough to condemn him as a heretic.

Forret and the others were taken to Castle Hill in Edinburgh, strangled and then burnt at the stake on February 28th 1540 (some sources give 1538 as the date). Tyndale had suffered the same fate near Brussels in 1536. But the spread of reforming ideas continued, and in 1543 under the Protestant-inclined regent, James, Earl of Arran, the Scottish Parliament passed an Act authorising the use of the Bible in the English language.

Rev. Dr Alison Peden

John Knox

(?1514 - 1572)

Over the centuries the church in Scotland, ruled by distant Rome, had become increasingly corrupt. The bishops were known more for political power and rich living than for their godliness. But there were some, throughout Europe, who sought to live a more biblical Christianity, and when in 1517 Martin Luther nailed his 95 theses to the church door in Wittenberg in Germany, the Reformation was born.

Around three years earlier, in a Scotland still mourning the loss of so many good men at the battle of Flodden, a son John was born to the Knox family in Haddington. It was he, more than any other, who brought the Reformation to Scotland.

Good at his studies, John Knox become a priest, and a private tutor in his home town. During that time, he came across the teaching of the reformers, notably George Wishart, a Scot who had brought the new ideas from Cambridge and from Germany. Knox became Wishart's bodyguard, standing in front of the pulpit with a sword in hand, but he could not protect him from the powerful figures in Scotland who objected to his teachings against the Church. In 1546 Wishart was captured, tried, and burnt at the stake in St Andrews Castle.

Only weeks later, a small band of men captured the Castle. Knox joined them, and was persuaded to preach, a powerful and pivotal moment, surrounded by men who knew they were risking their lives for this freedom. Besieged, they appealed for help to protestant England, but instead it was French ships which arrived, summoned by the Queen Regent, Mary of Guise. The Castle was taken, and, with others, Knox was sentenced to be a galley slave. For three years he endured the harsh conditions on the French galleys, steadfast in his beliefs in a living and righteous God.

At last Knox was released, and made his way to England, where he preached before the King, the protestant King Edward VI, and was made chaplain to the town of Berwick. The four years there were a period of calm and freedom when Knox became known as a powerful preacher. It was also where he met and married Majorie Bowes, daughter of a nobleman who certainly did not approve of the match. But to Knox, Marjorie was always 'dearlibelovit'; to others 'one of the very sweetest of women'.[1]

In 1553 the English King died, and his half-sister Mary Tudor came to power. The pendulum swung again, and Knox fled to Europe just before Queen Mary launched the persecution and execution of hundreds of protestant believers, including four eminent bishops.

Making his way to Geneva, where John Calvin was the influential leader in this centre of the Reformation in Europe, Knox settled in to a congregation blessed with clear-thinking and dedicated men. For a brief period he was invited to lead the small congregation of English protestant refugees in Frankfurt, but he clashed with members who wished to use the

A FRENCH GALLEY

English Prayer Book, while he wanted more freedom in worship. Leaving that congregation, he was aware that he would not now be welcome back in the English protestant church.

The years spent in Geneva, where Marjorie joined him, were happy times, with Calvin as his mentor and friend. He was invited to pastor the English Church in Geneva, while helping prepare a revised translation of the bible, and writing the *Book of Common Order* which later became much used in Scotland. But he kept in touch with friends in Scotland, and knew that there were many there 'who wished to break from the corruptions of Rome, hungry for a new and cleaner communion.'[2]

He always yearned to return to Scotland, to help lead the Reformation there, and he made several attempts to do so. His frustration at being thwarted by the actions of the female rulers of Scotland and England, (the Queen Regent and Mary Tudor) erupted in the *First Blast of the Trumpet against the monstrous Regiment of Women*, his most infamous piece of writing which lost him friends.

Mary Tudor died, and once more the balance changed. The protestant Queen Elizabeth I came to power in England. The Queen Regent in Scotland was still hostile, but the 'Privy Kirk', meeting in private houses, sent word to Knox to invite him to return. And on 2nd May 1559 he landed at Leith. Word quickly spread - Scotland was ready for change.

Knox immediately joined a gathering of preachers and supporters in Perth, summoned by the Queen Regent to answer charges. His fiery preaching against idolatry, tyranny and superstition, asking for freedom to speak the Gospel, stirred up many to action. It was said that 'the voice of one man is able in one hour to put more life in us than five hundred trumpets continually blustering in our ears'.[3] Churches were purged of symbols of Rome, monasteries were raided, and religious artworks, regarded as idols, were destroyed. The movement spread, and grew, despite skirmishes with the forces (Scottish and French) loyal to the Queen Regent, Mary of Guise.

The year 1560 brought resolution. After intense diplomacy by Knox to persuade the English Queen that it was in her interest to have a protestant neighbour, English troops arrived in Leith. Scottish leaders made a treaty with England, Mary of Guise died, the French troops went home, and the Scottish Parliament was returned to power. Then Knox, now minister of St Giles in Edinburgh, was asked to form the constitution of the Kirk of Scotland.

And so he did. At the same time as they passed acts to abolish the authority of the Pope throughout Scotland (and make the Mass illegal), the Parliament 'in free and lawful assembly' voted through the Confession of Faith and Book of Discipline drawn up by Knox. The Kirk was to be a democracy for everyone, with lay elders given equal voting rights with clergy, and an emphasis on 'right understanding, teaching and worship', with the Bible in English to be read by all. To this end, Knox advocated a school in every parish, and was instrumental in founding the University of Edinburgh, and Marischall College, Aberdeen. He also proposed that the huge wealth of the Roman church be divided equally between the Kirk, the poor, and the schools, with parish ministers taking responsibility for such things as poor relief, care of the sick and aged. (Over the next hundred years the schools were built, but the wealth went elsewhere.).

The following year Mary Stewart, Queen of Scots, returned to Scotland a young widow, from France. She remained true to the church of her mother, through all the political intrigues of the times, and this resulted in many verbal skirmishes with John Knox. She even had a charge of treason made against him - he was found not guilty by the Privy Council. But after six years as Queen, there was a rising against Mary and she was forced to abdicate in favour of her young son James.

The coronation of the infant King James VI took place in the Church of the Holy Rude, by Stirling Castle, on 29th July 1567. The preacher was John Knox, the Bible text from 2 Kings 11, the stirring sermon about another boy-king who 'did what was right in the eyes of the Lord'. And Scotland had a moment of security and peace, as the Parliament again ratified the establishment of the reformed church.

But as long as Mary Stewart still lived, there could be no peace in the country, and Knox continued to defend his Kirk from pulpit and desk right up to the end of his life. He was buried beside St Giles in 1572.

The Regent said at his grave 'Here lies one who never feared the face of man'.

A remarkable man, John Knox was one who shaped today's Scotland more than most. To quote a recent historian, 'Knox was a democrat. The ideal he gave Scotland as a legacy was of a democratic state, caring for its weakest members, with free education available to all, fiercely independent and with its own voice in Europe.'[4]

Dr Alison J. Wilkinson

* * *

For references please see the Notes section, part I.

George Buchanan

(1506 - 82)

George Buchanan became a towering national figure in his day. Rising from humble beginnings, he would eventually ascend to a position where he would rub shoulders with some of the most prominent members of European society and academia. A Latin scholar, historian, philosopher and humanist, Buchanan was a man of many talents, but throughout his life he would always hold fast to his strong Christian beliefs.

Buchanan was born in Killearn, the son of a farm owner. His father died at a young age, however, and Buchanan was only saved from a life of poverty by the timely intervention of his uncle, James Heriot of Trabroun, who funded Buchanan's education at the University of Paris from 1520. Buchanan quickly proved himself to be an able scholar, but the untimely death of his uncle meant that - unable to meet the cost of his university fees - he had no choice but to return from France to Scotland in 1522.

For a while he was engaged with the French Auxiliaries, but his military service was short-lived and he soon returned to his academic interests, graduating from the University of St Andrews in 1525. The following year he made his return to the University of Paris, receiving his Masters Degree in 1526, and was appointed Professor of the College of Sainte-Barbe in 1529.

Buchanan's academic record was exemplary, and he held a number of different posts within the University of Paris before taking up the post of tutor to Gilbert Kennedy, the Earl of Cassilis, in 1532. Five years later, Kennedy was to return to Scotland, and Buchanan followed him to discover a country rocked by religious upheaval. He became interested in the work of the Reformers, though initially his own support for their cause was subtle and muted. In the coming years he was to write verse which was heavily critical of the Franciscan Order, which infuriated many including Cardinal David Beaton. However, Buchanan's keen satirical eye was to prove pleasing to Scotland's monarch, King James V, who offered him the post of tutor to his young son, James Stewart.

By 1539, Buchanan's support for Reformation ideals led to his capture, along with many others. It took all of Buchanan's ingenuity to escape incarceration, and it was only with the utmost effort that he eventually managed to flee the country and take up refuge in France once more. There, he was to waste little time in putting his scholarly talents to good use, becoming installed as Professor of Latin at Bordeaux's Guienne College. He continued to embark on many literary projects during his time in Bordeaux, which included verse, dramas and Latin translation. The latter came to be especially well-regarded among his peers, with Buchanan's aptitude being recognised far and wide.

A few years later Buchanan made a return to Paris, taking up a prominent post at the Cardinal le Moine College, but in 1547 he was invited by André de Gouveia - Principal of the College of Guienne when Buchanan had worked there - to join him at the University of Coimbra in Portugal, along with a number of other leading academics of the time. Buchanan agreed, but Gouveia's new role as Principal at Coimbra was short lived: he died later in 1547. The Inquisition investigated the university and ultimately held Buchanan and a number of his colleagues on several charges, with Buchanan himself being accused of engagement in Lutheran practices amongst other accusations. During his trial in 1549, Buchanan defended himself vigorously and - although not sentenced until two years later - he managed to escape the death penalty. Instead of execution, he was held captive at a monastery in Lisbon with the purpose of the resident monks instructing him with corrective theological teachings. Never one to allow circumstance to curtail his natural scholarly merits, he continued work on his Latin translations while incarcerated until his release from the monastery in 1552.

Now free to leave Portugal, Buchanan travelled to England and shortly after returned to France, where he took up another academic post - this time at Boncourt College in Paris - before later resuming tutorial duties. But in the early 1560s, Buchanan made his return to his native Scotland, being appointed tutor to the young Mary Stewart in 1562. He enjoyed a good professional relationship with Mary Queen of Scots, which preceded a rapid rise through the echelons of Scottish society. Having joined the Reformed Church, he was a member of the General Assembly of the Church of Scotland from 1563, eventually being appointed Moderator in 1567. Meanwhile, he became Principal of the College of St Leonard's in St Andrews, which allowed him to continue his scholarly work.

Some years later, Buchanan was to take up one of his most famous roles when he became appointed the Royal Tutor to King James VI at Stirling Castle. Buchanan was a hard task-master, imbuing the young monarch with a rigorous education which would stay with him throughout the rest of his life, even although James was to sharply deviate from the content of Buchanan's teachings (particularly with regard to the older man's contestation of the divine right of kings) in later years.

Simultaneously with his tutoring duties, Buchanan took up a number of offices of state, culminating in his appointment as Keeper of the Privy Seal of Scotland. His political and academic reputation now assured, he spent the closing years of his life working on what were to become arguably his two most prominent scholarly achievements, a treatise on the monarchy entitled *De Jure Regni Apud Scotos* (*The Powers of the Crown in Scotland*) in 1579, and a comprehensive history of Scotland (*Rerum Scoticarum Historia*) in 1582. He died shortly after completion of what was to be a landmark historical work, and was interred in Edinburgh.

Buchanan may be a figure of Scottish national history, but he was an intellectual with a truly international reputation. Author of a great many works and translations during his lifetime, his scholarly and literary output continues to inspire readers to this very day.

Thomas A. Christie

King James I and VI

(1566 - 1625)

What do Stirling and the Authorised Version of the Bible have in common?

Answer: King James VI!

Exactly four hundred years ago the famous version of the English language Bible commissioned by James VI of Scotland and I of England was published. It became the world's most famous Bible, selling billions of copies.

Stirling was one of James' favourite places in Scotland. In 1566 he was baptised in the old chapel royal in Stirling Castle. In 1594 James had the present Chapel Royal built for the baptism of Prince Henry, his firstborn son. Sadly, Henry died aged eighteen. James' second son, Charles I, who succeeded him in 1625, was baptised, not in Stirling, but in Holyrood Abbey.

James is famous for two great achievements. First, he brought Scotland and England together into a united kingdom. Second, he gave the English-speaking world its Bible.

The King James Bible was not the first. William Tyndale's New Testament in English began to circulate clandestinely in Scotland around 1527. A group of church leaders wrote from Stirling to John Knox in 1557 saying that it was their intention to read the Scripture lessons in

English. Previously church readings of the Bible were in Latin. Scottish churches favoured the Geneva Bible – so-called because it was translated by English-speaking exiles in the Swiss city.

However, the Geneva Bible was not popular with James because its marginal notes were critical of 'the divine right of kings.' So no doubt, when attending the General Assembly of the Church of Scotland meeting in Burntisland in 1601, James noted with interest the Assembly's desire for a new Bible translation. And when, shortly after becoming King of England, he convened a conference at Hampton Court Palace in 1604 to resolve tensions within the Church of England, he responded positively to Puritan John Reynolds' proposal that a new translation be made. This translation was published in 1611 and became known as the Authorised Version or the King James Bible.

With the passing of time the new version grew in popularity until it came to be universally recognised as 'the noblest monument of English prose.' Over its 400-year history the King James Bible made a unique contribution to the English language, to English literature, and to western culture.

Language: countless idioms passed into English through the King James Bible, including 'to lick the dust' (Psalm 72.9); 'to fall flat on his face' (Numbers 22.31); 'the skin of my teeth' (Job 19.20).
Literature: William Golding's *Lord of the Flies*, John Steinbeck's *East of Eden* and John Milton's *Paradise Lost* are just a few of the many works of literature inspired in part or as a whole by the Bible.
Culture: Films such as *Apocalypse Now* and *Chariots of Fire* borrow their titles from the Bible. Others like *Shawshank Redemption* and *The Matrix* draw on biblical ideas.

James, who was crowned infant King of Scotland in Stirling's Church of the Holy Rude in 1567, died in London in 1625. Four centuries later, the Bible he commissioned still lives on in the language of the 700 million English speakers worldwide.

Rev. Dr Fergus MacDonald

James Guthrie

(1612 - 61)

'The Lord visit the people of Stirling once more with faithful pastors, and grant that the work of the people of God may be revived through all Britain, and over all the world.'

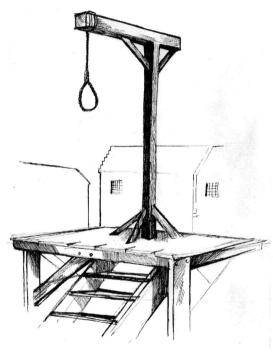

This prayerful wish was expressed towards the end of the lengthy speech made by James Guthrie from the scaffold before he was hanged on 1st June 1661. Despite his involvement in the national politics of church and state, his primary concern remained the gospel and the people of his parish of Stirling.

Although the Scottish Reformation took place in 1560, there were ongoing struggles within the Scottish church for more than a century. Many of these were linked to political conflicts between England and Scotland. In 1638, James Guthrie, the son of an Angus landowner and graduate of the University of St. Andrews, was appointed as the parish minister at Lauder. However, before he was inducted, Guthrie signed the National Covenant, against bishops in the Church of Scotland, the interference of the king in the church and the introduction of the English prayer book. Guthrie is said to have passed the hangman on his way to Greyfriars Kirk for the signing but carried on, despite knowing this action might eventually lead to his death.

In 1649, Guthrie moved to the Church of the Holy Rude in Stirling, where he was known as a great preacher and his 'Christianity was never blurred and vague'. He had a reputation of kindness to friends and servants and the Stirling manse was known as 'holy, happy and healthy'. However, he was also active in the national church and saw it as his duty 'to preserve and defend the true religion'. When Oliver Cromwell gained power in England, there was common ground between the Scottish protesters and the puritans, but still some differences. Because of his refusal to compromise, Cromwell described Guthrie as 'the short little man who could not bow'. To his friends and supporters, Guthrie was known as Mr. Sickerfoot (sure of foot).

As one of the authors of an inflammatory pamphlet entitled 'Causes of the Lord's wrath against Scotland', Guthrie was arrested in 1661. Appropriately for a man who did not hold back in his use of words, the indictment included the charge that Guthrie 'did contrive, complot, counsel, consult, draw up, frame, invent, spread abroad or disperse - speak, preach, declaim or utter divers and sundry vile seditions and reasonable remonstrances, declarations, petitions, instructions, letters, speeches, preachings, declamations and other expressions tending to the vilifying and contemning, slander and reproach of His Majesty, his progenitors, his person, majesty, dignity, authority, prerogative royal, and government'.

As he ascended the scaffold, Guthrie passed his ring to his niece. It was passed down through six generations of daughters of Church of Scotland ministers and is now held by the Smith Museum and Art Gallery in Stirling. Then, in his final speech, he said:

'In all these things which are the grounds of my indictment and death, I have good conscience, as having walked therein according to the light and rule of God's word, and as did become a minister of the gospel.'

Alan Kimmitt

* * *

For related sources please see the Notes section, Part II.

THE CHURCH OF THE HOLY RUDE, STIRLING

Robert Leighton

(1611 - 84)

You could call Robert Leighton a 'Presbyterian Bishop'. In the midst of bitter conflicts in the seventeenth century, Leighton was a voice of moderation, inspiration and holiness.

Leighton's father was persecuted in England for his strong Puritan condemnation of bishops. He sent his son Robert away to university in Edinburgh, and then to travel abroad. In France, he learned a lot from the Catholics who were following a reformed approach to faith. His passionate Christian commitment was both broadening and deepening.

Leighton became minister of the Kirk at Newbattle, near Edinburgh in 1641. He tried to encourage his flock to follow Christ more sincerely, by systematic visiting, good preaching and teaching on prayer and meditation.

Scotland was becoming ever more bitterly divided about church government, and Leighton resisted pressure to get involved: 'Since most ministers preach about current times, surely there's space for one who preaches about eternity?' But in the end, he signed the Covenant that bound Scots Presbyterians together – though he opposed violent enforcement of conformity.

As Principal of Edinburgh University in 1653, Leighton hoped to train holy and committed Kirk ministers. One student wrote, 'Mr Leighton taught me to be charitable to all good men of any persuasion'. He was Calvinist in his theology, but convinced that inner faith was much more important than outward forms, including Church government.

Hoping to reconcile warring factions in the Scottish Church, Leighton became bishop of Dunblane in 1661, seeing the role as guide and mediator. He remained unworldly and generous, tolerant and encouraging, but both sides rejected his moves. Charles II refused to accept his resignation, and promised conciliation for the Covenanters.

As Archbishop of Glasgow from 1670, Leighton again tried to make peace from a humble standpoint. Again, his hopes were dashed, and he resigned four years later, saying, 'I have done my utmost to repair the temple of the Lord.'

Leighton's faith always led him to hope rather than despair. He once preached, 'Go as the world will, my sin is forgiven me. Mistake me, accuse me who will, my God has acquitted me in his Christ, and he loves me, and lives to intercede for me'. Travelling to London for one last try at peace-making, he fell ill with pleurisy in an inn and died. He was 74 years old.

Death held no terrors for Leighton: 'I have a good hope, and a great desire to see what they are doing on the other side, for of this world I am heartily weary.' He always wanted to die on a journey, as a symbol of life as a pilgrimage towards God.

His large collection of books both Protestant and Catholic was left to the clergy of Dunblane whose ministry he had tried so hard to foster, and now forms 'The Leighton Library'. His Commentary on the First Letter of Peter has never been out of print since the late seventeeth century, and his other writings have inspired Christians from all denominations.

THE LEIGHTON LIBRARY, DUNBLANE

Leighton's hope was that Christians might see that it is the faith that they share, rather than the differences that divide them, which is really important. He summarised his teaching thus:

Remember always the presence of God.
Rejoice always in the will of God.
Direct all to the glory of God.

Rev. Dr Alison Peden

* * *

For further reading relating to this chapter please see the Notes section, part III.

Ebenezer Erskine

(1680 - 1754)

Ebenezer Erskine came from a godly family, and learned as a boy the importance of standing by your beliefs as he saw his father imprisoned for his faith.

His first conflict with the authority of the Church of Scotland was in 1722, when he was a minister in Portmoak, Kinross-shire. He wrote an important theological work called, 'The Marrow of Modern Divinity'. This work upheld a key Christian belief that salvation comes only by faith in Jesus Christ.

In 1731 Ebenezer moved to the West Church in Stirling. Two years later his name was further blackened in the eyes of the church authorities when he attacked publicly the practice of patronage. This practice whereby a land-owner had the right to appoint a local minister had led to many abuses such as bribery and nepotism.

Ebenezer, along with friends, was suspended from the church, and they constituted themselves as a separate church, the Secession Church.

Even in his own church he found himself embroiled in further controversy over his support for 'The Burghers' Oath', an oath of loyalty

THE ERSKINE MONUMENT

to the religion of the realm, which some felt would compromise their Christian conscience.

One memory which undoubtedly helped him to believe God had work for him to do, however many difficulties he faced, came from his beginnings. It was said he and his brother were born after their mother's death. When she was still a young woman, his mother became very sick, and died. Before she was buried her family asked that a much-loved family ring be removed from her finger , but due to the swelling of her finger this proved impossible. After the mourners had left the churchyard the sexton, who coveted the ring, opened the coffin and began to cut off the corpse's finger, whereupon she sat up and screamed!

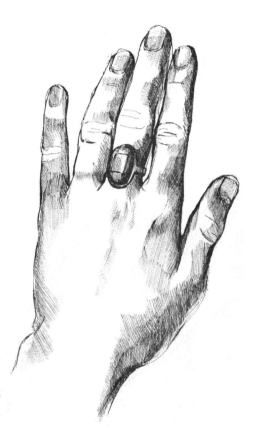

She then made her way home to where the mourners were gathered. The story goes that her husband, hearing a knock on the door, said to the company, "That knock! I would swear it was my dear wife Margaret's knock". One can hardly imagine the joy and amazement of those assembled.

This story, apparently far-fetched, is well attested by several sources.

Ebenezer was a man who found himself, against his will, caught up in different controversies within the church, but, like his father before him, he remained true to his beliefs.

Fiona Black

Robert Haldane

(1764-1842)

Robert Haldane was born as the eldest of three children into an aristocratic Scottish family on the 28th of February 1764 in his father's house in Cavendish Square, London. He had a younger sister who died in childhood. He also had a brother, James, who was born in Dundee, on the 14th of July 1768. Tragically his father had died just two weeks before the birth of his younger brother.

After the death of her husband his mother decided to live in Dundee. Being a committed Christian and from a family of Christians, faith was a central part of her life. She ensured that her three children were brought up to know God and to learn Bible truth. She did this while showing them all the love children without a father needed. On becoming a widow her chief concern was bringing up her two sons and daughter as Christians. She stressed to them the importance of eternity, particularly impressing upon them the need for clear Bible understanding. She also stressed the need for them to commit to memory and understand Psalms and portions of the Bible. This training in the Bible and need to understand scripture never left either boy throughout their adult lives. Years later, Robert Haldane described his mother and her influence in the following words '*she lived very near to God and much grace was given to her*'. His brother James said of his mother, '*My mother died when I was very young, I believe I was under six. Yet, I am convinced that the early impression made on my mind by her was never entirely removed and to this as an eminent means in the hand of God and left me with an inheritance which can never fade away*'.

Mrs Haldane died in 1774 after a cold which she caught on a visit to Crieff. Robert, the eldest was only 10 and was scarcely old enough to fully appreciate the extent of their loss. The children then stayed with their grandmother, until again, tragedy struck and she died in 1777. Thereafter, the boys were sent to board at the High School of Edinburgh.

On leaving school Robert Haldane entered the Navy, a choice which was made for him as his uncle was an Admiral of the Fleet. He served on several ships, all of which saw action against the French and on which he showed great courage in battle. He was 19 when peace was signed in 1783 and this brought to an end his short but active career in the Royal Navy. He stayed on in Portsmouth and became friendly with a local minister, Dr Bogue, whose long conversations with Robert reawakened his faith. Later he described how after the death of his mother spiritual things had played much less of a role in his life. However Dr Bogue had reconnected him with the truths he had learned from his mother.

On leaving the Navy, Robert came back to Edinburgh and went to study at Edinburgh University. In the summer holidays he would go on European grand tours as were the fashion of the time and went to Germany, Austria, Holland and always to Italy where he particularly liked Venice.

In 1785, aged 21, on his return from one of these trips he met and married Catherine Oswald, who was then only 18. Although both young their marriage proved to be long and happy, lasting nearly 57 years. Catherine proved to be a true helper in all Robert's future plans and unusually for the time was very involved in all the decisions he made. In September 1786 they moved to Stirling and settled at the old house at Aithrey Estate in Bridge of Allan. This estate was part of the family inheritance passed down from his father. A year later, their daughter Elizabeth, their only child, was born.

For the next 10 years after his marriage, Robert's time was spent mainly in country pursuits, particularly in improving his estate and the surrounding grounds. He dammed a stream flowing off the Ochils to form the current Airthrey Loch. In the Airthrey Estate there were many fine old trees, but many had been planted in the wrong place. Therefore he started to move and transplant full-grown trees. This was a new thing which few people had ever attempted before. His experiments were generally successful and attracted a lot of interest.

Locals even started rumours that he was actually contemplating the removal of the old house to a new situation. Instead in 1791 he erected a new house, designed by Robert Adam. Mr Adam was the architect of the day and the new house which looked like a small castle was very much the fashion for new buildings.

AIRTHREY CASTLE

He also built a stone wall extending the four miles around the park and enlarged the gardens and built walkways through the woods, which cover the overhanging rocks and hills. He erected summer houses on some of the viewpoints within the estate; unfortunately these have now tumbled into ruins. However today you can still see the outline of one in particular which was built on the face of the cliff in the Hermitage Wood. It was constructed to look like a woodland retreat where a hermit could live. During its construction Robert Haldane was standing too near the edge while giving instruction. His foot slipped and he fell but managed to grab hold of a wooden post. Later he always referred to this as his "post for life".

Not content with the erection of the hermitage Robert Haldane decided, that as a joke, he would advertise for a real hermit who could actually live within it. Over 40 people applied for the job, one of whom was particularly serious and was not to be put off. He was ready to comply with all the conditions, including that he should never leave the wood. Eventually it was explained to him, much to his disappointment, that it was only a joke.

Something began to change in Robert Haldane and he became more serious and began to be unsettled by his life as the 'country gent'. The turmoil caused by the French Revolution caught his imagination, particularly the great moral and political changes which the revolution caused. It had come upon the rest of Europe like an earthquake, highlighting the corrupt aristocracy, a church and priesthood which was totally worldly and the cries of overtaxed ordinary people. Robert Haldane was immensely interested in these events happening all around him.

What caught his imagination was the prospect of a new and better order of things and that governments would be regulated with a regard for the welfare of the people. He refused to join any political parties or to be aligned with any particular cause. As a member of the aristocracy he had everything to lose in pursuing the ideas of revolution. However he was strongly attracted to the chance to change the existing order.

Many of his fellow aristocrats shunned him and openly criticised his views accusing him of becoming a revolutionary. His view was that he appreciated the heritage that his family name and fortune bestowed on him. However he saw them not as anything with intrinsic value, but as something which could be used for the benefit of others and for the country of Scotland, a theme that he later fully developed in his evangelistic endeavours.

At this time the other idea that gripped his mind was the work of the Baptist missionary William Carey and his pioneering work in India. He became increasingly keen to go to India with his brother and Dr Bogue. The idea was pursued and plans were made. The one thing that the whole project depended on was getting permission from the East India Company. Unfortunately, they flatly and consistently refused all approaches to granting access to India. Even using his many powerful aristocratic contacts within Government and the Establishment made no difference. At the time the East India Company saw Christianity only in terms of potential disruption amongst the native people. Being interested only in profit, they saw that his missionary work would only unsettle the Hindu workforce.

On finding the door firmly closed Robert Haldane wondered if instead God was leading him in another direction closer to home. He then started working with his brother James to spread the news of God's love to the people of Scotland. Together they started the Tabernacle Church in the New Town of Edinburgh. From this base, James and Robert travelled throughout Scotland as itinerant preachers. They visited many towns and villages where their message was met with great interest and large crowds. They circulated Bibles and tracts as well as training young men as preachers and church workers. They also started Sunday Schools and funded the building of small churches.

In some towns this work was met with great opposition, for example in North Berwick the provost hired a brass band to march up and down and the other side of the field to where the brothers were preaching in an attempt to disrupt their meetings.

In order to fund their blossoming work Robert decided to sell the Aithrey Estate. It took nearly two years to sell, during which time Robert continued to fund the work from his own pocket. The proceeds of the sale of the estate amounted to £25,000, which in today's money amounts to approximately £20 million. With this money, the brothers agreed to erect churches in all the chief towns of Scotland and to fund a major increase in the number of evangelists they were sending out across Scotland.

As well as this work in Scotland, they also organised for groups of young African orphans to be brought to Scotland for adoption and to give them a full education before they went back to Africa as future leaders.

This work was seen to be radical and it generated much opposition and criticism from the established church. This opposition lasted throughout the rest of the brothers' lives and they were forced to fight what at times were nasty and vicious smears against their names.

In 1816 Robert Haldane, wearied by some of these battles, decided to visit Geneva. On arriving there, he found that there was effectively no Protestant church. He then met by chance a group of theological students. These students were eager to hear him speak and he subsequently had many meetings and conversations with them. Another aristocratic Christian, Henry Drummond, joined him in Geneva, and together they preached to large numbers of people over a period of months. Their preaching is credited with forming the basis for a revival in the City with many people giving their lives to Christ.

On returning to Scotland, Robert continued to support the growing evangelistic work. However, he spent more of his time writing and reading. Two themes in particular took more and more of his time. Firstly, helping work with the Bible Society, he became concerned as to a lack of a clear spiritual reason why the Apocrypha should be included in the Bible. Secondly, through his reading and studies, he came to feel that there was no sound Christian exposition of Paul's letter to the Romans. The impact of his arguments against the Apocrypha being included in the Bible has been credited as being one of the major reasons why it has since been removed from today's modern Bibles. His work on Romans took many years to complete, but it was finally published in 1840 shortly before his death in 1842, aged 78.

Robert Haldane's legacy is immense in terms of evangelising and church planting in Scotland. However it cannot be looked on as only his efforts as so much of his work was done with his younger brother James. It was together that they worked as team, Robert providing the finance and organisation and his brother the preaching and teaching. Today there are many church congregations which owe their original existence to these extraordinary men. The tens of thousands of souls who were won for the Kingdom of God is their eternal legacy. Robert Haldane's last words in many ways sum up the man and his approach to life 'Forever with the Lord... for ever... for ever'.

To honour this remarkable man, in 2005 a group of local Christians formed The Haldane Trust to fund Christian youth work in the Stirling area and beyond. The Trust now has two full time workers working in local schools and churches. It has also developed links to a Christian school and orphanage in India where young people from Scotland spend time helping work with those less fortunate than themselves.

Kenneth Ferguson

The Drummond Family

(1793 - 1888), (1799 - 1877), (1851 - 97)

The eminent Drummond family have become a well-known part of Stirling history, and their contribution to spiritual life has been significant not only to the local area but also to the wider world.

William Drummond (1793-1888) was a prominent land surveyor, nurseryman and evangelist in nineteenth-century Stirling. Along with his brother Peter Drummond (1799-1877) and nephew Henry Drummond (1851-97), he ensured that his family would become responsible for the furtherance of God's Word in a variety of different ways.

Aside from their extensive business concerns, the Drummond family invested in the exploration of continental Africa (an area of immense interest at the time) and the formation of a celebrated museum of agriculture. However, the most recognised demonstration of the

Drummonds' commitment to spreading the Good News proved to be their establishment of the Drummond Tract Enterprise in Stirling, in the year 1848. This famous institution was founded by Peter Drummond, a seed merchant by trade. A member of the Free Church, he made use of the Enterprise to create a range of pamphlets which highlighted issues of interest to Christians, including the robust defence of moral values and the encouragement of spiritual revival.

The impact of the Drummonds' efforts was far-ranging. They led a successful campaign to halt the Stirling Races (held annually in the King's Park until they were disbanded in 1853, on account of the drunkenness and social disorder that regularly resulted from them), while other early pamphlets argued vigorously to uphold the sanctity of the Sabbath Day and to promote a lifestyle that was in keeping with Biblical teachings.

By the end of the 1850s, the Drummond Tract Enterprise had made available a range of nearly two hundred different publications, which in total had led to the circulation of some eight million individual copies. The publication of books and pamphlets with a religious theme was popular from the mid-nineteenth century onwards, but the Drummonds' company quickly established itself as a leader in the field. Over the decades their range of publications and capacity for circulation went from strength to strength, beyond the confines of the United Kingdom and into the expanding British Empire. Such was the public demand for Drummond publications that rail links to and from Stirling had to be extended in order to cope with the increasing need for regular shipments of printed matter. By the beginning of the twentieth century the Drummonds were producing not only instructional writings on theological issues, but also fiction with a Christian theme and a variety of stories for children. Several of these publications had print runs of many tens of thousands of copies, paving the way for the emergence of regular religious magazines and journals.

While Peter Drummond eventually turned to evangelism full-time, his brother William dedicated himself to continuing to run the family businesses, all of which were to remain prosperous over the years ahead. However, Henry Drummond was to prove that the family's devotion to evangelical matters would live down through the generations.

Henry studied science at Edinburgh University, where he showed aptitude in a number of different disciplines, but ultimately he made the decision to become a minister of the Free Church. This choice would prove to be a discerning one, for a few years later he was appointed a lecturer in the field of natural science at the Free Church College - a post which would allow him to combine his scientific abilities with his religious enthusiasm.

Some years after he entered the college's employ in 1877, Henry Drummond published what was almost certainly the most significant work of his career, *Natural Law in the Spiritual World* (1883). This text impressed both theologians and scientists alike, and was to lay the foundation for many later works which explored issues such as missionary movements and evangelical matters; they included *The Ascent of Man* (1894) and *The New Evangelism and Other Papers* (1899), the latter collection being published posthumously after Henry's death in 1897.

The Drummond family's influence can still be seen in Stirling today, including the imposing building of Old Viewforth - a grand mansion house in Pitt Terrace constructed for Peter Drummond in 1855 - which currently accommodates the administrative headquarters of Stirling Council. Yet few would deny that the Drummonds' most enduring architectural legacy lies in the Valley Cemetery. William Drummond was responsible for the creation of the famous Star Pyramid, one of the most recognisable structures in this famous graveyard which is situated close to Stirling Castle. Commissioned from monumental sculptor William Barclay in the year 1863, the Pyramid is replete with inscriptions of titles from many Drummond Tracts and contains a copy of the Holy Bible sealed within its structure. It stands today as a testament to the Drummond family's lifelong commitment to the propagation of religious principles, their deep respect for printed matter, and their celebration of the Christian way of life.

With their vast catalogue of publications and undeniable international prominence, the Drummond family established themselves at the very forefront of Christian activity throughout the nineteenth and twentieth centuries. Not only did they accomplish their ambition of spreading the philosophy of Christian values throughout the globe, but in so doing - and with such overwhelming success - they also brought prosperity to Stirling at large, making their company virtually synonymous with the production of religious tracts. It is testament to their enduring significance that Drummond publications remain of academic interest to literary scholars and theologians more than a century and a half after their initial release.

Thomas A. Christie

Robert Murray McCheyne

(1813 - 43)

Robert Murray McCheyne was a young man from Edinburgh who became the minister of St Peter's Church in Dundee when he was only 23 years old in 1836. Although he died in 1843, his ministry is very famous. A book by his best friend Andrew Bonar entitled *The Memoir and Remains of Robert Murray McCheyne* became a best seller and McCheyne is known all over the Christian world because of his work and the revival that took place in Dundee. If you want to learn more about him then I have written a book called *Awakening* which tells his story in a way that I hope you will find interesting and stimulating. What I would like to share with you just now is some of his work before he went to Dundee – here in Larbert and Dunipace.

DUNIPACE PARISH CHURCH

On the 7th of November 1835 McCheyne was ordained and inducted as an assistant to the minister, John Bonar. It was a fascinating parish for McCheyne to be involved in. Larbert and Dunipace could lay claim to being the first industrial parish in Scotland due to the establishment there of the Carron Ironworks in 1759. In 1835 the community itself was in a period of rapid growth – the population had increased from 400 in 1790 to 6,000 in 1835. This included over 2,000 industrial workers.

However the growth in the population and increasing prosperity meant that there was an increase in drunkenness and a general decline in public morality. Religion, whilst not unimportant, was in proportionate decline. Services were held every week and membership in the church increased to several hundred. In Larbert there was the unique problem of men who had been slaving over hot fires all week, finding the church too cold!

The week after his induction McCheyne wrote, 'Today I am going to visit from house to house'. Much of his time in Larbert was to be spent doing this. It was something that he greatly enjoyed and excelled in. Although at the beginning he struggled with questions of relevance and how to relate to the people, he learnt quickly. He sought to use illustrations, to be simpler in his speech and to press home the spiritual lessons he taught. Social conditions at the time were grim. He records that one third of the sick he visited died, many within a day of his first visit.

He kept detailed systematic records of where he visited and what he did in each home. These make really interesting reading – here are a couple of examples - 'Major Dundas is a curious mixture of a character. He is an Elder, most attentive at Church, – visits the sick – has family prayers – talks a great deal about religion – plays the guitar – sings – tells absurd stories – in short a puzzle. Mrs Dundas is a deep sea – gracious and condescending – professes great religiousness – is full of whim and conceit – she has two little daughters 11 and 12 – who glide in like fairies most elegantly dressed". Writing to his parents in the summer of 1836 he records his impression of a visit to an elderly woman – "she is the worst melancholy monument I ever saw. She is so deaf that she says hardly anything can make her hear. She is so blind that she cannot read – and she is so cold and careless that she does not want to know. And she is so old that she will very soon die – I suspected that she made herself more deaf than she was in reality and therefore tried to make her hear. She knew that Jesus had shed his blood. But when I asked her why? She said that "really her memory was so bad she did not know but her husband used to be a grand man at the books!'"

He also learned quickly when it came to preaching. There were five preaching stations around Larbert and so McCheyne preached three times on Sunday and several times during the week at Bible classes and meetings. Whereas Bonar preached for one and a half hours, McCheyne usually preached for 'only' 35 minutes because he thought the people could not stand much more. His sermons were simple and concentrated on the basic doctrines of the Christian faith.

One other aspect of McCheyne's work in Larbert was his work amongst young people. The 22 year old minister started classes for young people. In these he used his musical and artistic abilities to good effect. His aim, as he told his parents, as to 'entertain them to the utmost, and at the same time to win their souls.' He succeeded in gathering a group of sixty young people. He had a genuine empathy and love for young people. An example of this is a letter he wrote to a teenage boy who was looking for work – 'I do not know in what light you look upon me, whether as a grave or morose minister, or as one who might be a companion or friend; but, really, it is so short a while since I was like you, when I enjoyed the games which you now enjoy, and read the books which you now read, that I can never think of myself as anything more than a boy. That is one great reason why I write to you. The same youthful blood flows in my veins that flows in yours – the same fancies and buoyant passions dance in my bosom as yours – so that when I would persuade you to come with me to the same Saviour, and to walk the rest of your life "led by the Spirit of God," I am not persuading you to anything beyond your years. I am not like a grey-headed-grandfather – then you might answer all I say by telling me that you are a boy. No: I am almost as much a boy as you are; as fond of happiness and of life as you are; as fond of scampering over the hills, and seeing all that is to be seen, as you are.' Using his artistic and musical gifts with the young was something McCheyne was keen to develop.

He was only in Larbert eleven months and yet for McCheyne these were crucial for his forthcoming ministry in Dundee. What he had learnt in Edinburgh he was able to practise in Larbert and Dunipace. We too can learn from him today.

Rev. David Robertson

LARBERT OLD CHURCH OF SCOTLAND

Christian McLagan

(1809 - 1901)

Christian MacLagan was an exceptional and determined Victorian woman. Her father died when she was nine and the family moved into Stirling from a farm near Denny. Her main interest was Scottish history. History was to her as real and vibrant as the autumn colours of the beech, oak, and ash that grew along the Back Walk below the Castle.

Following in her father's and grandfather's steps she developed a keen knowledge of archaeology and antiquities (ancient works of art). She studied, recorded, and drew very many ancient items ranging from Iron Age Forts and Brochs (Scottish drystone roundhouses/towers) to Pictish picture stones, and cairns. This passion was to last throughout her unusually long life, but sadly she is little known. Although she contributed enormously to the understanding of archaeology and published widely, her work was not taken seriously by academic groups of the time, simply because she was a 'mere woman'. It especially rankled that her gender stopped her from being elected a *Fellow of the Society of Antiquaries of Scotland:* it was of little consolation that she was listed as one of its six 'Lady Associates'.

Christian was educated at home along with her two brothers and sister. At this time education was limited to the rich, and in Stirling it was not until 1880 that schools accepted girls as well as boys. Although there were no public libraries in the town when Christian was young, she probably had access to the fine library of her mother's relatives in Shropshire, or to those of her ministerial grandfathers'. She was proficient in Latin, Greek, Gaelic, French and perhaps Italian, and despite a deformity of the bones in her right hand, of which she was extremely self-conscious, she was also an excellent artist.

Christian's family was fairly wealthy so she did not have to work, but she was never idle. Her time was spent, as a companion to her widowed

mother at the family home in Pitt Terrace, promoting education in Stirling, improving the town's appalling housing, and supporting her local church. Following her mother's death in 1858, Christian built her own house in Clarendon Place, whilst she used some of the rest of her inheritance for Christian outreach work. She was instrumental in setting up the Marykirk (1868) on St Mary's Wynd in the Top of The Town, as a mission charge in connection with the Free North Church in Murray Place.

Christian outlived all her immediate family. An independent woman of means, she dedicated much of her time and energy travelling far and wide, from Bennachie to Brittany, from St. Andrews to Sardinia, cataloguing and drawing many of the ancient monuments she feared were rapidly deteriorating. Across the Scottish countryside frost and rain were weathering and destroying some, while others were being plundered and ransacked by local people using the stone for their own building work. Christian must have been aware that the stones for the impressive local sixteenth century building Mar's Wark, at the top of Broad Street, were taken from Cambuskenneth Abbey, and that Mar's Wark itself only remained because it was an effective windbreak for the street below.

For a woman, even an educated one who published four books and many papers, the path to academic acceptance was rocky. Lauded and supported by some, she was ignored by many others. Her main contribution was a large book entitled *The Hillforts, Stone Circles and other structural remains of ancient Scotland*. One of her most ardent academic admirers was a fellow archaeologist and also a Christian believer, Sir James Y. Simpson, who was Queen Victoria's obstetrician and who first introduced chloroform as an anaesthetic for use in childbirth. Regardless of her well known supporters and her proficiency as a pioneering field archaeologist, historian and writer, Christian MacLagan was blocked right, left and centre. Much fun seems to have been made of this unusual and independent woman who, if she did not have a measuring tape to hand, would quite readily put her umbrella to good use when recording the dimensions of any monument that caught her analytical and artistic eye.

Having her work rejected by the majority of her fellow academics was a huge disappointment, but it did little to dent her determination. Hoping not just to record the past but to inspire future generations of artists, Christian made an outstanding collection of rubbings of stone art work and gravestones from the Bronze Age to the Sixteenth Century. Lacking recognition in Scotland, and perhaps in a fit of pique, she donated most of this collection to the British Museum in London (they are now held in the British Library, London).

Christian MacLagan is a little remembered yet remarkable woman: her grave can be seen in the Valley Cemetery beside the Church of the Holy Rude. It is a plain polished granite slab with only the inscription 'Christian', in Greek of course, as befits an exceptional academic of her time.

Rev. Mairi Lovett

Annie Croall

(1854 - 1927)

Six battles which changed the course of Scottish history took place in and around Stirling. For the most part, these were bloody, decisive and short. A seventh battle which by comparison lasted a lot longer and is very little known, is that waged by Annie Croall. She set up, ran and kept solvent, the Stirling Children's Home.

Annie Croall was the daughter of Alexander Croall, first curator of the Smith Institute. The necessity of having a children's home in Stirling became apparent, when, coming down the Back Walk to the Smith Institute one night in 1873, she found an abandoned baby. Its mother had gone into the town for drink and got herself arrested. A passionate Christian, Annie had been attending an evangelical meeting in the upper town that night.

Annie Croall had an uphill struggle to establish and maintain a home for children in Stirling. She had an even harder task convincing outsiders of the necessity of such a place, for few middle class people in Stirling and elsewhere understood the social mess and misery caused by living in a barracks town where prostitution was rife and children were often an unwelcome by-product. Men were sent off to war and families were left to fend as best they could. Annie Croall found children who

were abused, beaten and starving, she found toddlers left to fend for themselves on scraps in common lodging houses, and she took in babies born in stables in St Mary's Wynd, or on the Gowan Hill. She raised children and had them repatriated in Canada.

To do this, she had to become a first class publicist, fund-raiser and general manager. She was good at all those things. She managed to secure a three page article in 1901, in the very first issue of *The Ladies Review of Reviews*, a short lived Scottish woman's magazine published in Glasgow.

Also in 1901, after 25 years experience of running the home, Annie Croall published *Service on a Scottish Battlefield*, followed by *Fifty Years on a Scottish Battlefield* in 1923. She must have reflected frequently on the two day  duration of Bannockburn, compared with her fifty year struggle, and sought to catch attention for her cause by making the comparison. Ultimately, the whole town was involved in the cause, and names and addresses are entered in the annual reports against every sum of a shilling and over. The highest amount she ever received was £200, on two rare occasions.

Stirling Children's Home functioned from about 1876 to 1980 when it was taken over by the Aberlour Child Care Trust. The Home lasted over 100 years, accommodating and caring for Stirling's children. Unlike children's homes elsewhere, with conditions exposed as harsh and exploitative in retrospect, the testimonies from Stirling are of a loving, caring environment.

A contemporary of Annie Croall called her 'A Mother in Israel' in recognition of the pioneering Christian work which she undertook for Stirling's children.

Dr Elspeth King

George Yuille

(1845 - 1935)

Long ministries can be either the sign of continuous effectiveness or of refusal to change. George Yuille served as minister of Stirling Baptist Church for forty-three years (1870-1913). They were years of progress, change and growth allied to an outlook which was world-wide in scope. When he came to Stirling, his first and only Church, the membership was 100. When he left it was 216. He impressed by his enthusiasm, his wide interests and his evangelistic zeal.

He was born in Irvine in 1845 in a home greatly influenced by one of the early spiritual movements in Scotland and, during his ministry in Stirling he was profoundly influenced by a similar revival movement in Wales in 1904. He worked to bring that same renewal of spiritual life to Stirling. Through advertising in the local press, working with other ministers and other Churches, particularly the East Parish Church, through vigorous evangelism using well-trained lay leaders and through a varied programme of public lectures, his activities led to a marked growth in the Baptist community.

He was not averse to change. During his ministry non-alcoholic wine was substituted for alcoholic wine at Communion Services and the use of a hymn book was introduced to replace the singing of Psalms only in worship. His horizons went far beyond Stirling. He tirelessly supported the Baptist work in Bohemia and such was his support of the Baptist cause in

OLD STIRLING BAPTIST CHURCH (DEMOLISHED 1988)

Saskatchewan that Estevan Baptist Church renamed itself Stirling Baptist Church.

He made his mark in the wider circles of Baptist life in Scotland. He encouraged the Baptist Churches in the central belt to co-operate more closely. From 1880 till 1919 he was Secretary of the Baptist Union of Scotland which he had helped to form and which body he also served for three years as the Superintendent of its Home Mission. In the last years of the nineteenth century, he edited the *Scottish Baptist Magazine* and in 1926 he edited the *History of the Baptists in Scotland.* Described as 'orthodox but fair' he argued for historic Christology at the Baptist Union's one heresy trial in 1932.

His wife, Jessie, was also an influential woman. She identified herself with the suffragette movement and in 1905 was the leader of the local branch of the Woman's Social and Political Union. She was also prominent in the Stirling branch of the British Woman's Temperance Association. Her best known ministry was in support of the Zenana Mission. This Mission worked among Hindu women in India who lived in Zenanas closed to conventional missionary activities. She also became one of the most prominent leaders of the Women's Auxiliary of the Baptist Union of Scotland. The *History of Stirling Baptist Church* states that Jessie Yuille 'stands out in Scottish Baptist ranks as a most remarkable woman and probably the most influential female leader in the denomination in the early part of the 20th Century.'

Together this minister and his wife, based in Stirling, had a wide and influential ministry.

Rev. James Taylor

Elizabeth MacLean

(1854 - 1923)

Mrs Elizabeth MacLean seemed an unlikely candidate for the Suffrage Movement. She was the wife of Rev. Ebenezer MacLean, a Free Church minister who had retired early for health reasons. They moved from Banffshire to Stirling and settled in Clarendon Place. They had a comfortable lifestyle, with a cook and housemaid to attend to their needs.

Mrs MacLean was not content to 'sew a fine seam' and sip tea in her drawing room with her friends. From her window she could look up towards the Top of the Town - the district surrounding the Castle. She soon discovered that this was an area of great need. Some of the houses were crumbling; there was overcrowding and poor sanitation. Unemployment and alcohol abuse compounded the situation. The castle was a military barracks and drunken revelry and

A VENNEL, TOP OF THE TOWN

unwanted pregnancies were not uncommon in the neighbourhood.

In these days there was no Welfare State - no council housing, no National Health Service, no sickness or unemployment benefit.

As an active Christian, Mrs MacLean could not ignore the situation. She joined the *Stirling Female Society for the Relief of Aged and Indigent Women*. The members raised funds and then distributed cash and bags of coal to single and widowed women with no other access to aid. While visiting the homes, in her role of District Visitor, Mrs MacLean became well acquainted with the desperate living conditions that existed.

Realising that heavy drinking was the cause of much misery in families, Mrs MacLean became active in the British Women's Temperance Society, serving on the local committee alongside Mrs Jessie Yuille of the Baptist Church, who was president.

Aiming to encourage good nutrition in the home, Mrs MacLean regularly published her recipes in the Temperance News, under the name of Auntie Lizzie. These were so popular that she compiled a *British Women's Cookery Book* in 1905. This is one of her recipes:

Clarendon Roll

1 lb steak minced with ¼ lb fat bacon	*pepper and salt*
½ teacup of milk	*2 teacupfuls of bread crumbs*

Mix all together with the hand in a basin and pat out into a roll; lay it on a baking pan and stick some little bits of dripping over it; sprinkle with bread crumbs; bake in a smart oven for three quarters of an hour. This is nice eaten cold cut in thin slices.

Auntie Lizzie

However, Mrs MacLean and her friends realised that more would be required to free working women from oppression. They reckoned that if women had the vote then they could support the abolition of alcohol, among other reforms. The members of the local Temperance Society voted in favour of Women's Suffrage. They became active participants and Mrs MacLean and Mrs Yuille shared the platform at a Stirling meeting with the eminent Suffragist leader, Mrs Emmeline Pankhurst.

The Suffrage movement was well supported in the Stirling area by both men and women. In 1908 the Stirling Observer reported a meeting in the Albert Hall with 2000 people crammed inside and another 1000 trying to get in.

THE ALBERT HALL, STIRLING

As Suffrage and politics were closely connected and the Liberal Party was considered the party of reform, Mrs MacLean became very involved in the Women's Liberal Party, acting as its treasurer. Sir William Campbell-Bannerman, who became Liberal Prime Minister (1905-08), represented the Stirling Burghs in Westminster for forty years. He was regarded as sympathetic in principle but inactive in practice towards Women's Suffrage. Mrs MacLean would doubtless have availed herself of every opportunity of a word in his ear regarding the plight of his constituents and the right of the Cause.

When the Suffrage movement became militant and aggressive in character, Mrs MacLean and Mrs Yuille withdrew from public office: they considered prayer to be a more potent weapon. At the time the *Daily Mail* was credited with changing the name of the participants from Suffragists to Suffragettes, indicating the change in campaigning tactics. Two incidents were reported in Stirling - one of vandalism within the

Wallace Monument, and another a personal assault involving pepper and a dog-whip upon Herbert Asquith, the current Prime Minister, who was strongly opposed to votes for women.

Mrs MacLean did not live to celebrate the passing of the Equal Franchise Act in 1928. She died in Bridge of Allan, aged 69 years. She was in many respects an ordinary housewife, but she believed the Christian principle that all are equal, and she lived her life trying to bring justice and mercy to the poor.

Margaret L. Lovett

Chapter Notes

I. John Knox

1. Elizabeth Whitley, *Plain Mr Knox*, p.53 Scottish Reformation Society ©1960
2. Elizabeth Whitley, *Plain Mr Knox,* p. 87 Scottish Reformation Society ©1960
3. Gordon Donaldson, *John Knox: Scotland's Great Reformer*, p.15 Pitkin ©2000
4. Roderick Graham, *John Knox: Democrat*, p.354 Robert Hale Ltd ©2001

* * *

II. James Guthrie

- Jock Purves, *Fair Sunshine: Character Studies of the Scottish Covenanters.*
- J. H. Thompson, *The Martyr Graves of Scotland.*
- Alexander Smellie, *Men of the Covenant.*
- Ian B. Cowan, *The Scottish Covenanters 1660-88.*

* * *

III. Robert Leighton

- D. Butler, *The life and letters of Robert Leighton* (Hodder and Stoughton, London 1903)
- O. Chadwick, 'Robert Leighton after 300 years', *Journal of the Society of the Friends of Dunblane Cathedral'* XLV.iv (1985), 116-126
- J.M. Allan, *'Only my books...' Bishop Leighton's bequests* (University of Stirling Bibliographical Society, Occasional Publications 5 (1985)
- K. Brown, 'Reformation to Union', in eds. R.A. Houston and W.W.J. Knox, *The New Penguin History of Scotland* (2002), pp.182-275.

Further Reading

Bellesheim, Alphons, *St Columba and Iona: The Early History of the Christian Church in Scotland* (London: Eremitical Press, 2010).

Brewster, Lynn, *Suffrage in Stirling: The Struggle for Women's Votes* (Stiring: Monument Press, 2002).

Devine, T.M., *The Scottish Nation: 1700-2007* (London: Penguin, 2006).

Donaldson, Gordon, *Scottish Kings* (New York: Barnes & Noble Books, 1993).

Donnachie, Ian, and George R. Hewitt, *The Birlinn Companion to Scottish History* (Edinburgh: Birlinn, 2007).

Dowden, John, *The Celtic Church in Scotland* (London: Elibron Classics, 2000) [1894].

Dunlop, Eileen, *Queen Margaret of Scotland* (Southport: NMSE Publishing, 2005).

Elsdon, Sheila M., *Christian MacLagan: Stirling's Formidable Lady Antiquary* (Brechin: Pinkfoot Press, 2004).

Fraser, Antonia, *The Life and Times of King James VI of Scotland, I of England* (London: Weidenfeld and Nicolson, 1974).

Goring, Rosemary, ed., *Scotland: The Autobiography*, 2nd rev edn (London: Penguin, 2008).

Herman, Arthur, *The Scottish Enlightenment: The Scots' Invention of the Modern World*, rev edn (London: Fourth Estate, 2003).

King, Elspeth, *Old Stirling* (Catrine: Stenlake Publications, 2009).

King, Elspeth, *Stirling Girls: Towards a Women's History of Stirling* (Stirling: Stirling Smith Art Gallery and Museum, 2003).

Lang, Andrew, *John Knox and the Reformation* (London: BiblioBazaar, 2007).

Magnusson, Magnus, *Scotland: The Story of a Nation*, rev edn (London: HarperCollins, 2001).

Marshall, H.E., *Scotland's Story* (Tenterden: Galore Park Publishing, 2006) [1906].

Marshall, Rosalind K., *John Knox* (Edinburgh: Birlinn, 2008).

Moffat, Alistair, *Before Scotland: The Story of Scotland Before History* (London: Thames and Hudson, 2009).

Moffat, Alistair, *The Faded Map: The Story of the Lost Kingdoms of Scotland* (Edinburgh: Birlinn, 2010).

Murray, Iain H., *A Scottish Christian Heritage* (Edinburgh: The Banner of Truth Trust, 2006).

Oliver, Neil, *A History of Scotland* (London: Orion, 2009).

Oram, Richard, *David I: The King Who Made Scotland* (Stroud: The History Press, 2008).

Osler, Douglas, *The Way It Was: Norman Invasions: Queen Margaret of Scotland* (Edinburgh: Chambers, 1978).

Pagan, Anne, *God's Scotland?: The Story of Scottish Christian Religion* (Edinburgh: Mainstream Publishing, 1998).

Renwick, A.M., *The Story of the Scottish Reformation* (Fearn: Christian Focus Publications, 2010) [1960].

Scott, Robert, and Alasdair Hogg, *The Way It Was: The Middle Ages: David I: A Medieval King* (Edinburgh: Chambers, 1978).

Tranter, Nigel, *The Story of Scotland*, rev edn (Glasgow: Neil Wilson Publishing, 1992).

Winn, Christopher, *I Never Knew That About Scotland* (London: Ebury Press, 2007).

Websites of Interest

Scotland's History
http://www.ltscotland.org.uk/scotlandshistory/index.asp

Scottish Christian History
http://scottishchristian.com/category/history/

The *Gazetteer for Scotland* History Time-Line
http://www.scottish-places.info/timeline.html

The Online History of Scotland
http://www.scotlandhistory.co.uk/

Scottish History Online
http://www.scotshistoryonline.co.uk/

Robert M. Gunn's *The Story of Scotland*
http://skyelander.orgfree.com/scotland.html

Scottish History
http://www.scottishhistory.com/

All About Scotland
http://www.visitscotland.com/guide/scotland-factfile/

A Timeline of Scottish History
http://www.rampantscotland.com/timeline/timeline.htm

In Search of Scotland
http://www.bbc.co.uk/history/scottishhistory/

The *Undiscovered Scotland* Timeline of Scottish History
http://www.undiscoveredscotland.co.uk/usfeatures/timeline/to1000.html